Günter Gerngross
Herbert Puchta

Join Us
Pupil's Book
for English

Contents

2

CAMBRIDGE
UNIVERSITY PRESS

C000051010

Hello friends!

1   **Listen. Sing the song.** ♫ English is easy ♪

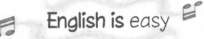

English is easy,
Come on and join in.
English is easy,
Let's begin.

Are you ready, kids?
Yeah!
OK. Join in:

Sandwich, hamburger, hot dog,
Pullover, cowboy and jeans.
Cinema, Walkman, snack bar,
Taxi, clown and superstar.

Well done, everybody. See you tomorrow.

Bye-bye, Miss Williams.

2 Listen and act.

Who's your best friend?

Mary Jones. She's in my class.

Who's your best friend?

Nick Brown. He's in 3B.

Look!

This is Emma. **She's** my friend.

she's = she is

This is Mike. **He's** my friend.

he's = he is

3 Read and write. Listen and check.

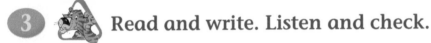

Emma, who's your best friend?

Emily. ....'s in my class.

Mike, who's your best friend?

Mark. ....'s in my class.

4   Listen and sing. ♫ The numbers rock ♫

1, 2, 3, 4, 5, 6,
7, 8, 9, 10, 11,
12, 12, 12, 12 o'clock.
Do the numbers rock.

5 Look and colour the numbers.

11 15 20 9 18 19

8 12 17 2 13 5 1

6 10 16 7 4 14 3

one   two   three   **four**   five   six   **seven**   eight   nine

ten   eleven   twelve   **thirteen**   fourteen   fifteen

sixteen   seventeen   eighteen   **nineteen**   twenty

five   5

6 Listen, point and repeat.

10 20 30 40 50

| ten | twenty | thirty | forty | fifty |

7 Listen and find the colour. Then circle the number.

23
(27)

46
49

33
31

22
28

29
27

34
39

41
47

50
53

45
42

8 Guess, count and write.

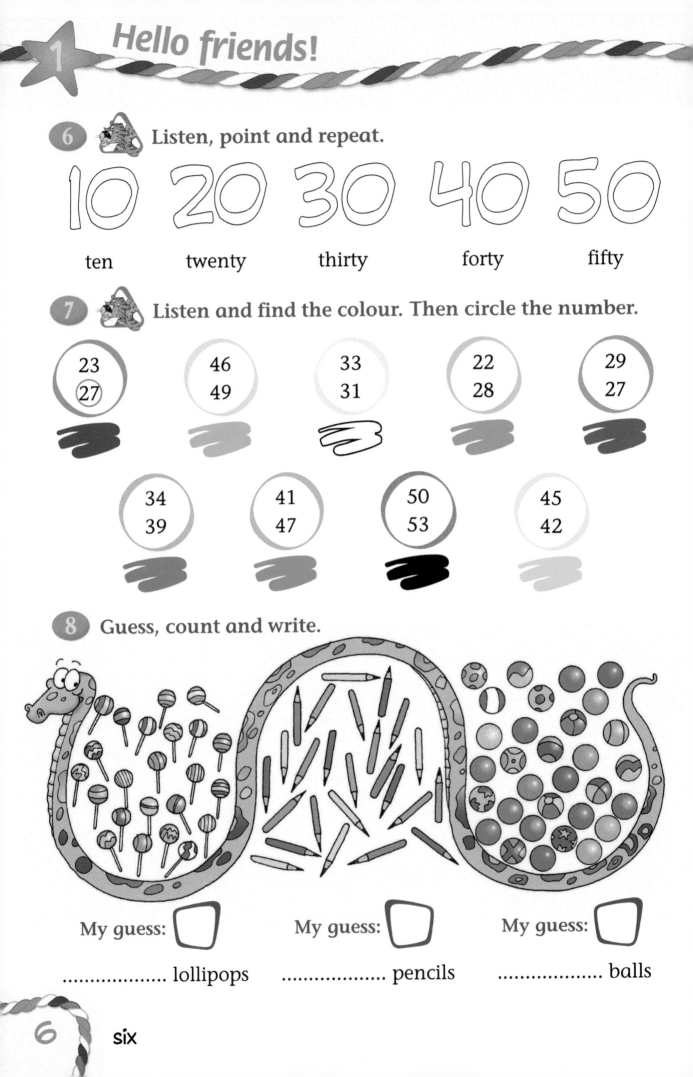

My guess: ☐

My guess: ☐

My guess: ☐

.... lollipops

.... pencils

.... balls

Listen and act.

Hi, what's your name?

Alice. What's your name?

John. How old are you?

I'm eight.

Are you in 3B?

Yes.

Is Mr Brown your teacher?

No, he isn't.

Is Mrs Lucas your teacher?

Yes, she is.

Look!

Is Mr Brown your teacher?
No, **he isn't**.

Is Mrs Lucas your teacher?
Yes, **she is**.

10 Listen and read the story - The snails.

11 **PROJECT TIME** - Make a number snake.

12 **WRITING** - Write your favourite numbers. Then play Bingo.

Bingo

Numbers:
| 3 | 8 | 12 | 17 | 33 |

My favourite numbers: three, eight, twelve, seventeen and thirty-three.

Check your English!

WORDS Write the words.

24 ....

46 ....

50 ....

37 ....

22 ....

30 ....

SENTENCES Write *He* or *She*.

1 This is Emma. ....'s in my class.
2 This is Maria. ....'s my friend.
3 Mike is my best friend. ....'s in 4B.
4 This is Jimmy. ....'s great!

TEXT Complete the text.

is – numbers – friend – and

My favourite .... are nine, seven, twelve .... twenty.
My best .... is Toby. English .... easy.

My progress

Good!   Very good!   Excellent!

1  **Listen and write the numbers.**

2 **Read and write the numbers.**

- ○ board
- ○ floor
- ○ desk
- ○ chair
- ○ light
- ○ door
- ○ cupboard
- ○ wall
- ○ glue
- ○ ceiling
- ○ scissors
- ○ window

3 Read and colour.

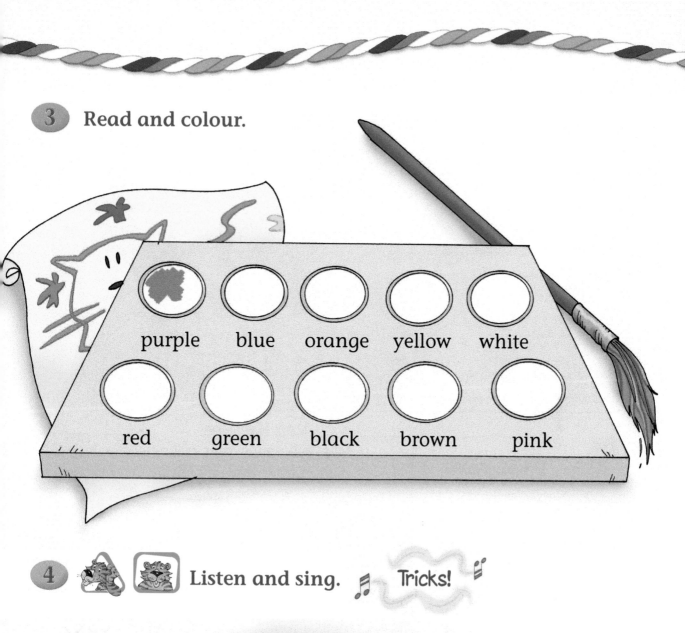

purple   blue   orange   yellow   white

red   green   black   brown   pink

4  Listen and sing. ♫ Tricks!

I'm Magic, the magical cat!
I play tricks on Pit and Pat.
I like to eat and play
And I sleep a lot every day.
Abracadabra, wizzy woo
Let me show my tricks to you!

5 Listen and read the story - The magic tree.

6 Complete the dialogues.

7 Listen. What colour is Pit's bag?

8 Play the memory game (page 77).

9 Look and complete.

The cupboards are orange.

The door is blue.

The board ....

The desks ....

The .... yellow.

The .... brown.

10  Listen and mime.

Hello, everybody.
I'm Toby
the tiger.

12 PROJECT TIME - Play the game.

13 WRITING - Write about your classroom.

My classroom

White walls, brown chairs,

green desks, an orange door,

two blue cupboards.

Check your English!

WORDS Write the words.

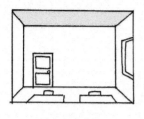 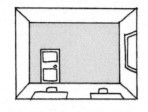 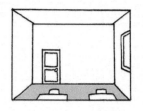

....

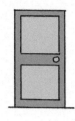  

....

SENTENCES Match.

1 What's in the box?   Here you are.

2 What colour is your bag?   Good morning.

3 The scissors, please.   A pen and a ruler.

4 Good morning.   Brown and green.

TEXT Complete the text.

I'm - teacher - name - in

My .... is Mary. .... eight.

I'm .... 3B. My .... is Mrs Richardson.

My progress

 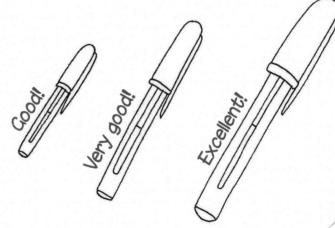

Good! Very good! Excellent!

School in the UK

We have assembly in the morning.

Hello! Welcome to our school.

This is the playground.

This is the school canteen.

Other children bring a packed lunch.

Some children have school dinners.

This is an art lesson!

A science lesson in the park.

In the summer we have a Sports Day.

running race

sack race

This is a photo of our school play.

About me

This is my best friend Emily. And this is her family.

1  Listen, point and repeat.

Mum

Dad

sister

brother

Grandma

Grandpa

My brother's name is Peter,
my mum's name is Dee,
my dad's name is Ronald,
my name is Emily.

My grandma's name is Rita,
my grandpa's name is Lee,
my sister's name is Sandy
and that's my family.

Hey, that's my family,
my family,
my happy family!
That's my family,
my family,
my happy family!

2   Listen and sing.  Happy family

3 Listen, point and repeat.

happy   **tired**   **angry**   **sad**   **thirsty**   **hungry**

4 Listen and draw.

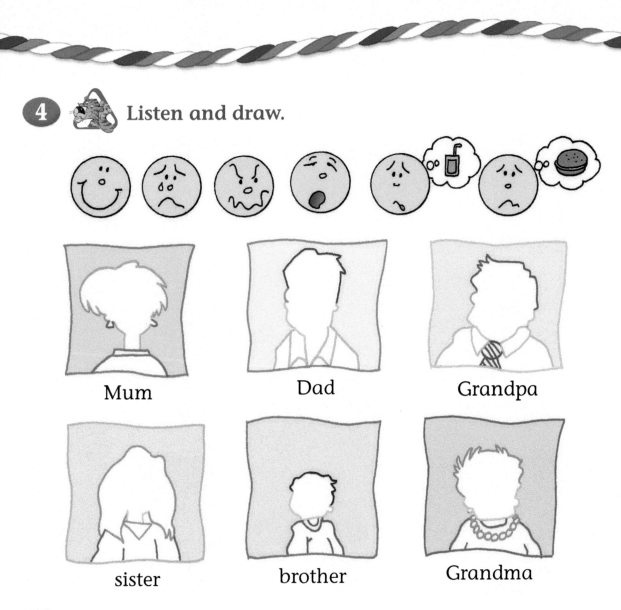

Mum

Dad

Grandpa

sister

brother

Grandma

5 Play the mime game.

3

6 Listen and read the story - The birthday present.

Oh dear.

I'm sorry, Dad. The game isn't stupid. I'm not angry now.

That's OK, Mike.

Let's play the game.

Good.

7 Listen, point and repeat.

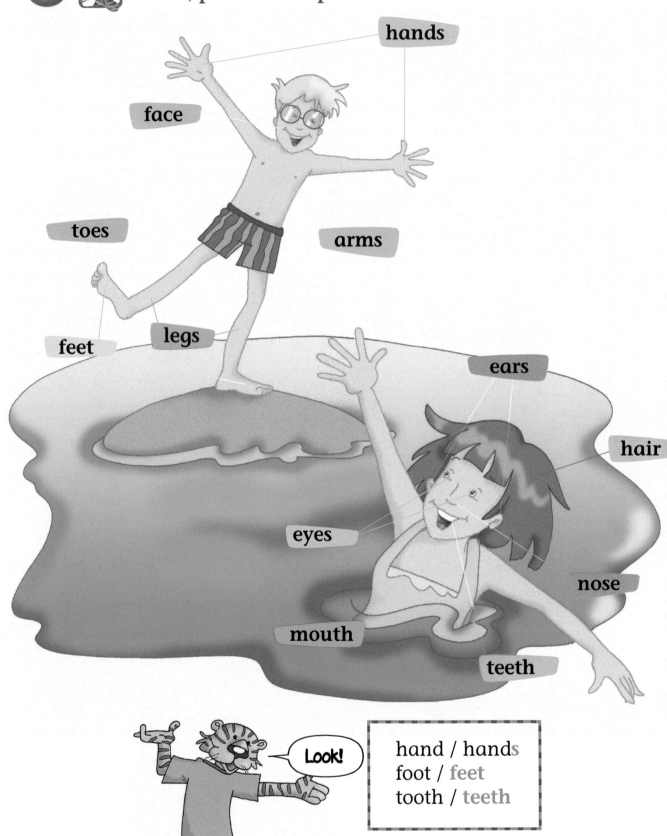

hands

face

toes

arms

feet

legs

ears

hair

eyes

nose

mouth

teeth

Look!

hand / hands
foot / feet
tooth / teeth

8   **Listen and sing.** 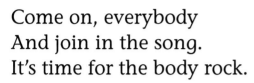 The body rock

Come on, everybody
And join in the song.
It's time for the body rock.

Shake your hair.
Touch your ears.
Shake your legs and touch your feet.
Touch, touch, touch, touch your nose.
Now come on, touch your toes.

Shake your hands.
Touch your face.
Open your mouth and show your teeth.
Touch, touch, touch, touch your nose.
Now come on, touch your toes.

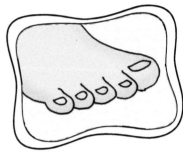

Now read and colour the frames.

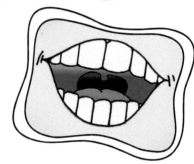

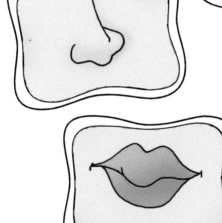

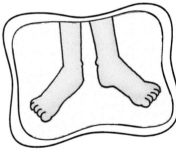

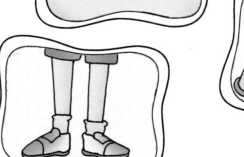

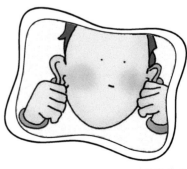

About me

9  Listen and colour Priscilla the pirate.

Hi, I'm Patty the parrot.

10 Look and write.

a **big** nose

a **small** nose

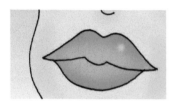 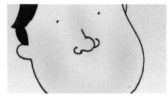 

a .... mouth   a .... nose   .... ears

 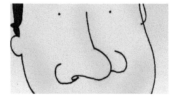 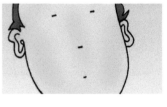

a .... mouth   a .... nose   .... ears

Look!

a small nose
a pink mouth

green eye**s**
big ear**s**

30   thirty

11 **Listen and write the names: Jim, Harry, Rob and Bill.**

....

12 **Read, look and write the numbers.**

Captain Black

Captain Flint

1 He's got a red nose, a small pink mouth, small ears, brown arms, big hands and small feet.

2 He's got a red nose, a big mouth, small ears, brown arms, small hands and small feet.

3 He's got a pink nose, a big red mouth, big ears, brown arms, big hands and big feet.

4 He's got a pink nose, a big red mouth, small ears, brown arms, big hands and small feet.

Look!

 He's got black hair.  She's got brown hair.

13 **PROJECT TIME** - Play the game.

> What about Emily's mum?

> Is she tired?

> Is she sad?

> No, try again.

> Yes.

14 **WRITING** - Write about your family.

My brother Tom

This is a photo of me with my brother. His name is Tom.

He's ten. He's happy here.

He's got a new book.

Check your English!

WORDS Write the words.

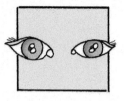
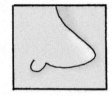
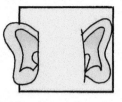

....

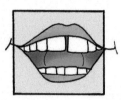

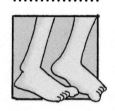

....

SENTENCES Match.

1 Happy birthday!   That's OK.

2 I'm sorry, Dad.   Yes, she is.

3 Are you tired?   No.

4 Is she angry?   Thank you.

TEXT Complete the text.

hair - a - eyes - nose - teeth - big

He's got black ...., green ...., ... big
...................., yellow .... and .... ears.

My progress

Good!

Very good!

Excellent!

4 Let's eat and drink!

1 Listen, point and repeat.

I like breakfast.
I like lunch.
I like dinner.
Munch! Munch! Munch!
There are many things I like to eat:
chips and pizza, fruit and meat.
I really love my favourite dish.
What is it? It's fish!

ice cream

mineral water

bananas

milk

apples

chicken

chips

fish

cheese

pizza

bread

popcorn

orange juice

hamburgers

spaghetti

2   Listen and sing. I like to eat

 34   thirty-four

3 Speak.

I like fish. I don't like chicken.

I like spaghetti. I don't like pizza.

4 Listen and draw the mouths.

Susan

Simon

Brenda

Derek

Julia

Bruce

5 Listen and read the story - Bad luck for Pat.

6 Listen and say the chant.

 Do you like apples? No, I don't.

 Do you like milk? No, I don't.

 Do you like pizza? No, I don't.

Do you like? What do you like? Ice cream, ice cream, I love ice cream.

7 Ask three friends. Draw the mouths.

Do you like fish? Yes, I do.

Do you like cheese? No, I don't.

:) :(	Name:	Name:	Name:
(fish)	:)	:)	:)
(cheese)	:)	:)	:)
(apples)	:)	:)	:)
(chicken)	:)	:)	:)

8 Solve the puzzle. Complete the sentences.

Maria   Rosie   David   Julia   Simon

Maria likes bananas.
Rosie likes spaghetti and ....
David likes apples and ....
Julia .... cheese.
Simon ....

9 Listen and check.

10 Write.

Christine

Mario

Christine's favourite food is fish.
Christine's favourite drink is orange juice.
Mario's ....
Mario's ....

 **Look!**

I like ...

David likes ...   Maria likes ...
He likes ...   She likes ...

11 Listen and mime.

12 Listen and write the numbers.

13 Circle.

APPLESFISHCHIPSCHICKENPIZZACHEESEMILKBANANASBREADSPAGHETTIMINERALWATERHAMBURGERSORANGEJUICEICECREAM

14 Listen and write their favourite food.

Sally   Paul   Tom   Tina   Ben

p..............   s..............   f..............   h..............   c..............

15 Play the guessing game.

16 PROJECT TIME - Order some food and drink.

A hamburger, please.

Here you are.

Thank you.

You're welcome.

17 WRITING - Draw and write about your favourite food and drinks.

My favourite food

I like | I don't like | Favourite

I like chicken, chips and spaghetti.
I don't like cheese and popcorn.
My favourite food is pizza and
my favourite drink is milk.

Check your English!

WORDS Write the words.

....

....

SENTENCES Match.

1 Do you like fish?   You're welcome.

2 What's your favourite food?   Here you are.

3 An ice cream, please.   Spaghetti.

4 Thank you.   No, I don't.

TEXT Complete the text.

food - favourite - drink - don't - favourite - like

I .... chicken and spaghetti.

I .... like fish and cheese. My .... is pizza.

My .... is orange juice.

My progress

  Good!  Very good!  Excellent!

5 Free time

1 Listen, point and repeat.

1 play basketball   2 play the piano   3 skateboard   4 play football

5 swim   6 rollerblade   7 ski   8 ride a horse

Jimmy = he   Jane = she

Look!

2 Listen and tick. Say the answers.

Jimmy   Jane

Jimmy can ... and ... He can't ... Jane can ... and ... She can't ...

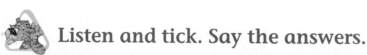

3 Write sentences about Jimmy and Jane.
Then write about your friends.

1 Jimmy can .... and ....

2 He can't ....

3 Jane can .... and ....

4 She can't ....

....

....

....

....

4 Ask a friend and tick the answers.

Vanessa, can you swim?

Can you ski?

Yes, I can.

No, I can't.

can

....
(name)

can't

Look!

| Can you ...? | Yes, I can. |
| | No, I can't. |

5 Free time

5 Listen and mime.

Oh, no!

6 Listen and write the numbers.

7 Solve the puzzle. Write *Yes* or *No*.

1 The boy in the red T-shirt and blue jeans can't play the piano and can't swim. He can ride a horse.

2 The girl in the white T-shirt and red jeans can't ride a horse and she can't rollerblade. She can play the piano.

3 The boy in the blue T-shirt and shorts can't play the piano and can't ride a horse. He can swim.

4 The girl in the pink T-shirt and blue jeans can't rollerblade and can't play the piano. She can ride a horse.

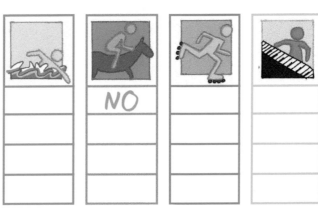

Sylvia		NO		
Terry				
Patricia				
Kevin				

8 Listen and read the story - At the park.

9 Write sentences about Laura.

Laura can ....

She ....

She can't ....

....

10 Write sentences about Harry.

Harry can ....

He ....

He can't ....

....

11 Solve the puzzle. Complete the sentences.

Jenny can ride a horse and swim.

Christina can rollerblade and ....

Ed can .... and play the piano.

John ....

Amy ....

12 Complete the sentences.

Toby can ....

He ....

Toby can't ....

....

13 PROJECT TIME - Play the game.

14 WRITING - Write about you.

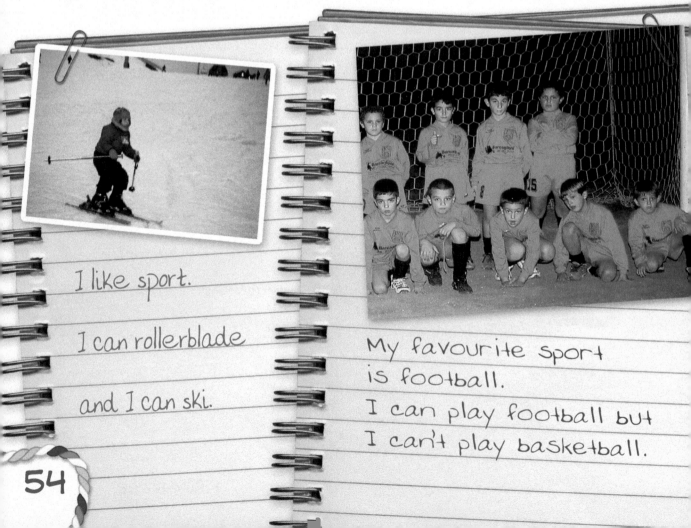

I like sport.

I can rollerblade

and I can ski.

My favourite sport
is football.
I can play football but
I can't play basketball.

Check your English!

WORDS Write the words.

....

....

SENTENCES Write the sentences.

1 the / He / play / piano. / can't

....

2 you / Can / ride / a horse?

....

3 new / I've / bow and arrow. / got / a

....

4 swim. / She / can

....

TEXT Complete the text.

can - She - you - swim - He

Peter can .... can't roller blade.

Laura .... play the piano. .... can't ski.

Can .... rollerblade or ski?

My progress

 Good!

 Very good!

 Excellent!

6 Animals

1  Listen and write the numbers.

○ lion

○ pig

○ cow

○ hippo

○ fox

○ wolf

○ sheep

○ rabbit

○ snake

○ duck

○ horse

2 Write the names of the animals.
Which animals are missing? ....

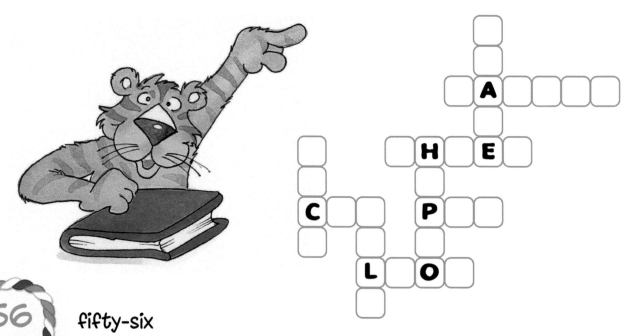

3 **Read and write. Listen and check.**

cow - sheep - rabbit - horse

1 It has got four legs.
It eats grass.
It lives on a farm.
It gives us wool.
It's a ....

3 It has got four legs.
It eats grass.
It lives on a farm.
It gives us milk.
It's a ....

2 It has got four legs.
It eats grass.
It lives on a farm.
You can ride on it.
It's a ....

4 It has got four legs.
It eats grass.
It's not very big.
It has got big ears.
It's a ....

4 **Read and tick. Say the sentences.**

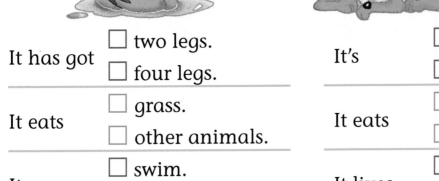

It has got	☐ two legs. ☐ four legs.	It's	☐ not very clever. ☐ clever.
It eats	☐ grass. ☐ other animals.	It eats	☐ small animals. ☐ grass.
It can	☐ swim. ☐ ski.	It lives	☐ on a farm. ☐ in the woods.
It's	☐ very big. ☐ not very big.	It has got	☐ two legs. ☐ four legs.

Look!

It	's = it is has got … lives in … eats …

Animals

6

5 Listen and say the chant. Then write the words.

Guess my animal, my favourite animal.
OK? Ready? Here we go!

Does it live in Africa?
No, no, no.

Does it live on a ....?
Has it got two ....?
Can it ....?
Can it ....?
Is it brown and ....?

I'm sorry, I'm sorry.
No, no, no.

It's not a crocodile.
Not an ....
Not a ....
Not a ....

It's a crocofrog!

dog

legs

cat

fly

sing

farm

elephant

red

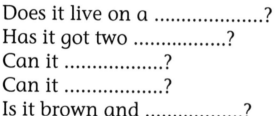

6 Listen and tick the answers. Then draw the animal.

Guess my animal.

No.

Can it fly?

	Yes	No
Has it got four legs?	☐	☐
Does it eat grass?	☐	☐
Does it eat other animals?	☐	☐
Is it a rabbit?	☐	☐
Is it big?	☐	☐
Does it give us milk?	☐	☐
Is it a ...?	☐	☐

7 Write the questions.

1 it / four / Has / legs? / got

....

2 on a farm? / Does / live / it

....

3 Does / other animals? / eat / it

....

4 it / eat / Does / grass?

....

5 green? / it / Is

....

6 hippo? / Is / it / a

....

8 Make questions.

1 [Does] [Has] it live on a farm?

2 [Is] [Can] it a tiger?

3 [Has] [Can] it got four legs?

4 [Can] [Has] it fly?

5 [Does] [Is] it eat grass?

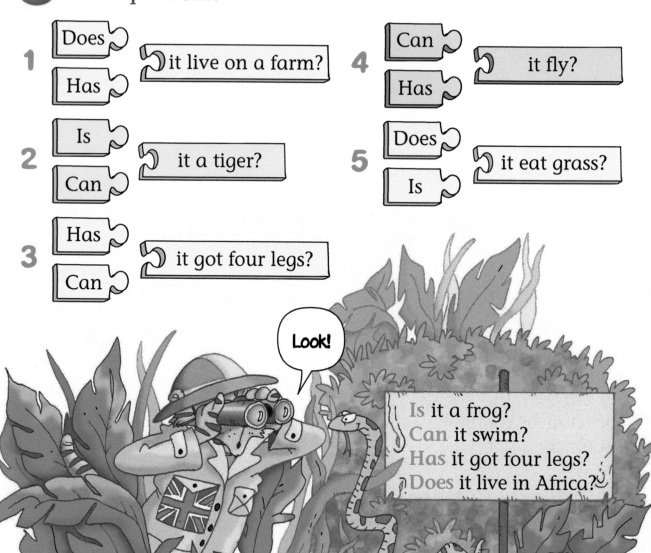

Look!

Is it a frog?
Can it swim?
Has it got four legs?
Does it live in Africa?

9 Complete the questions.

Can - Is - Does - Has - Is - Is - Has - Can - Is - Does

1 .... it got six legs?

2 .... it sing?

3 .... it brown and black?

4 .... it live in Africa?

5 .... it a lion?

6 .... it got big ears?

7 .... it fly?

8 .... it green?

9 .... it big?

10 .... it eat other animals?

10 Match.

It has got four legs.

It has got two legs.

It's brown.

It eats other animals.

It can fly.

It's green.

It's very big.

It's small.

It can roar.

It can sing.

11 Play the game.

Guess my animal.

Is it ...?
Can it ...?
Has it got ...?
Does it live ...?

sixty-one 61

Animals

12 Listen and read the story - The clever pig.

13 Listen and say the rhyme.

Clarissa Whiskers is a cat.
She eats a lot and gets quite fat.
One day she starts to swim and run.
And now she's fit and has more fun.

14 WRITING - Play the animal guessing game.

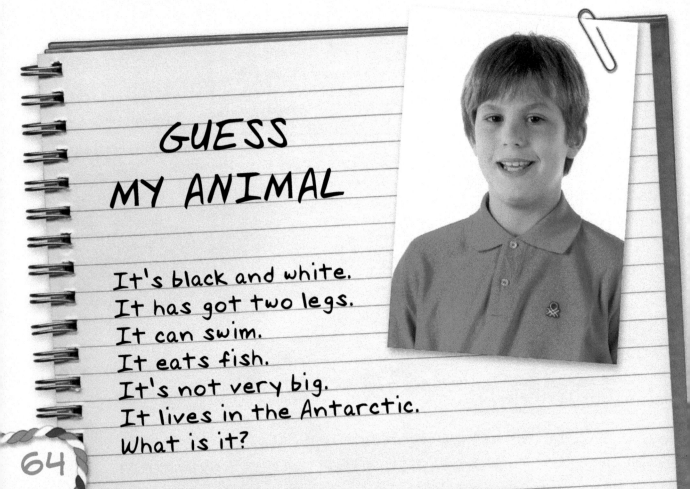

GUESS MY ANIMAL

It's black and white.
It has got two legs.
It can swim.
It eats fish.
It's not very big.
It lives in the Antarctic.
What is it?

Check your English!

WORDS   Write the words.

....

....

SENTENCES   Write the sentences.

1 has / It / four / got / legs.

....

2 live / Africa? / it / Does / in

....

3 it / got / legs? / six / Has

....

4 lives / farm. / a / on / It

....

TEXT   Complete the text.

lives - is - eats - has got - is - can - animal

It's a big .... It .... four legs and very big ears.
It .... in Africa and India. It .... grass.
It .... swim. It .... grey. It .... an elephant.

My progress

Good!

Very good!

Excellent!

LONDO

DAILY PROGRAMME

MONKEY GYM

See how they use their hands, feet and tails to survive in the rainforest.

TOUCH REPTILES AND SPIDERS

Are you brave? Come and touch snakes and spiders!

ZOO

There are 12,000 animals at London Zoo.

Many British children go on school trips to the zoo. There's a special programme for children everyday.

CAMELS AND THE DESERT

Learn how camels survive in the desert with little food and water.

FEED THE GIRAFFES

ee how giraffes eat.

PENGUIN LUNCH

Watch the penguins catch fish!

ELEPHANT ON SCALES

How much does an elephant weigh?

Halloween

1 Read.

Children have parties and dress up as ghosts, witches and monsters.

witch

They go from house to house and play 'trick or treat'. They ask for sweets.

At Halloween, people use pumpkins to make scary lanterns.

ghost

68 monster

pumpkin

Christmas

1 Listen and sing.

♪ Merry Christmas

In Britain people send lots of Christmas cards to their friends and family.

Merry Christmas
Merry Christmas
Father Christmas
is here.
Merry Christmas
Merry Christmas
And a Happy
New Year!

24th December

On Christmas Eve, before they go to bed, children leave a mince pies and a glass of milk for Father Christmas.

25th December

On Christmas morning they find lots of presents under the Christmas tree.

This is a Christmas cracker. It's fun to pull crackers with your family at Christmas dinner. Inside there's a paper party hat, a small gift and a joke.

2 **PROJECT TIME** - Make a Christmas puzzle.

1 Colour the Christmas puzzle.

2 Cut it out.

3 Stick it on cardboard.

4 Cut along the dotted lines.

5 Put the puzzle in a box. Wrap it.

6 Give it to a friend.

Easter

How many eggs can you find?

Unit 1 - Hello friends!

English is easy.
twenty
thirty
forty
fifty
What's in the box?
How many?
he
she
Who's your best friend?
My favourite number is 3.

Unit 2 - At school

board
floor
desk
chair
light
door
cupboard
wall
glue
ceiling
scissors
window
purple
Come here please.
Hurry!
Good morning!
Good night!
Here you are.
Stand up.
Stretch.
Clap your hands.
playground
art
science
lesson
race

Unit 3 - About me

family
Mum
Dad
sister
brother
Grandma
Grandpa
happy
tired
angry
sad
thirsty
hungry
Are you hungry?
face
arms
toes
legs
one foot/two feet
ears
eyes
mouth
one tooth/two teeth
nose
hair
I'm sorry Dad.
Is she angry?

Unit 4 - Let's eat and drink

breakfast
lunch
dinner
ice cream
mineral water
milk
bananas
chips
chicken
apples
fish
pizza

cheese
popcorn
orange juice
hamburgers
spaghetti
bread
I like chicken.
I don't like pizza.
I love hamburgers.
Christine's favourite food is fish.
Christine's favourite drink is
orange juice.
Do you like apples?
Yes, I do./No, I don't.
A hamburger, please.
You're welcome.
milk
cereal
chips
bacon
eggs
a cup of tea
toast
meat
vegetables
potatoes

Unit 5 - Free Time
play basketball
play the piano
skateboard
play football
swim
rollerblade
ski
ride a horse
Can you play basketball?
Jimmy can ride a horse.
He can't skateboard.
Turn off the alarm clock.
Put on your socks.
Put on your helmet.
Your turn Mike.

You're the winner!
duck
No, never.
My favourite sport is football.

Unit 6 - Animals
lion
pig
cow
hippo
fox
wolf
sheep
rabbit
snake
duck
horse
Does it live on a farm?
Has it got four legs?
Can it fly?
It eats grass.
clever
friendly
I'm scared!
Me too.
Stop it please!

Halloween
ghost
witch
monster
sweets
Trick or treat?
Go away!

Christmas
Merry Christmas!
Christmas tree
Christmas cracker
joke

Look!

Unit 1

This is Emma. **She's** my friend.

she's = she is

This is Mike. **He's** my friend.

he's = he is

Is Mr Brown your teacher?
No, **he isn't.**

Is Mrs Lucas your teacher?
Yes, **she is.**

Unit 3

hand / hand**s**
foot / **feet**
tooth / **teeth**

a small nose   green eye**s**
a pink mouth   big ear**s**

He's got   **She's got**
black hair.   red hair.

Unit 4

I like ...
David like**s** ...   Maria like**s** ...
He like**s** ...   She like**s** ...

Unit 5

Jimmy = **he**
Jane = **she**

Yes, I **can.**
Can you ...?
No, I **can't.**

Unit 6

It   **'s** = it is
      has got ...
      lives in ...
      eats ...

Is it a frog?
Can it swim?
Has it got four legs?
Does it live in Africa?

Memory game

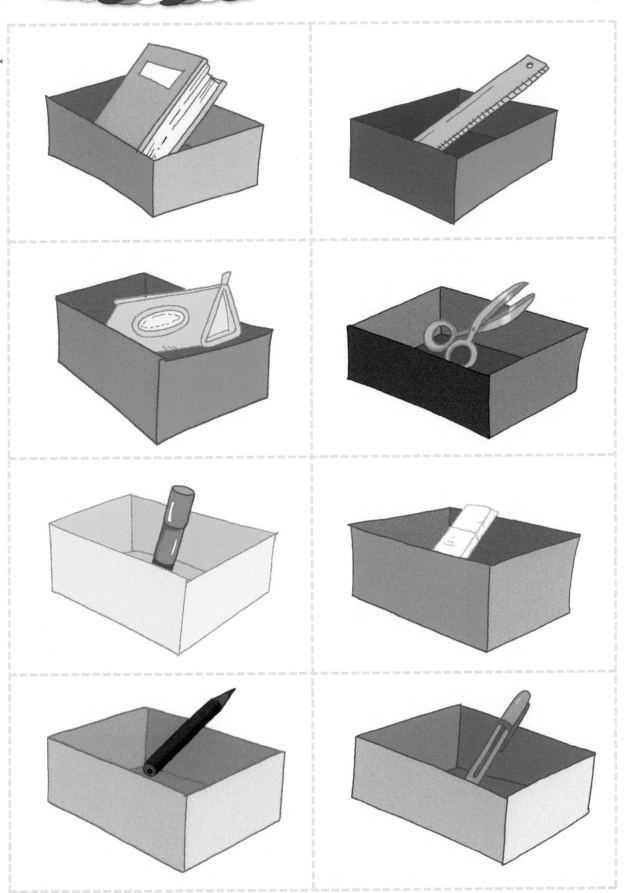

DIPLOMA

This is to certify that

....

....

has completed
level 2 of JOIN US

School ....

Teacher ....

Date ....

Well done!